The
Consequences
of
Slaughtering
Butterflies

Olaf Tyaransen

Acknowledgements are due to the editors of the following magazines in which some of these poems have previously appeared: The Word; Stet; Criterion '91; The Salmon.

Cover illustration by Toots
Back cover photograph by Nick Hitchcox
Printed by Nova Print

Special thanks to our patron Thermo King, Europe.

The author wishes to thank Keith Hopper, Anne Kennedy, Pat Ingoldsby, Jessie Lendennie, Michelle Quinn, Aidan Furey and Albert Hofmann.

ISBN 0 948339 89 6 Paperback only £4.50

Salmon Publishing, The Bridge Mills, Galway, Ireland

for my parents

Greetings and Salutations!
I'm absolutely delighted that
you're reading this as
I was becoming increasingly worried
that you would never come across
my name or my poetry
in your entire lifetime
- thereby defeating the purpose
of mine.

But now you have and
I'm happy
for both of us.

Contents

The Consequences of Slaughtering Butterflies

This morning I made
an assassination attempt
on a bothersome bee
and accidentally quoshed
a loitering butterfly
when my angry newspaper
smacked the window
killing all that flew
into its path.

Consequently Elizabeth exploded.
She screamed.
She shouted.
She pulled my hair.
She likes butterflies.
She stormed out of the room.
My day was ruined.
My life has been altered,
blown in new directions by
the flapping of a butterfly's wings.

I don't know how today
would have gone if it
hadn't gone the way it did
but looking on the bright side...
if I hadn't argued with Elizabeth,

we might have gone out for a drive
and been killed in a crash
instead of staying home throwing
pieces of the past
at each other.

So please accept my
deepest apologies for
ever writing this poem.
By putting pen to paper
I have caused you not to do
whatever it was you would have done
had you not been reading this.

I have affected your day
in many unknown ways
in much the same way
as the butterfly affected mine.

Maybe God just walked past the window
without interrupting
your reading.

Thoughts

Writing is one of the easiest things in the world.
Anyone can write.
Thinking is unavoidable.
Everybody thinks.
Everybody doesn't write.
Some do.
Many shouldn't
Some should but don't.
It is impossible to write without thinking.
It is easy to think without writing.
I think.
I write.
I think I should.
My thoughts are worth writing about.
I think.
Others read my work and think otherwise.
That is their privilege.
This is my vanity.
At least I have caused them to think why they don't
like my work.
Therefore my writing makes people think.
I can't lose.
What do you think?

My Entry to the Bewley's Poetry Competition

I'm sitting comfortably
by the window in Bewley's
with a mug of coffee
and the Irish Times.

I feel very secure
sitting here surrounded
by kitchen sounds, bored housewives
and ageing hippies.

There is an ad in
the paper - a picture
of a weak elderly African woman.
She looks near to death.
Underneath I am informed that
I can save her life
for a pound a day.

I look at my steaming
coffee cup. It cost fifty pence
(half a granny). Momentarily
I feel guilty.

I drink about
two lives worth of coffee
per day
in Bewley's.

But because Bewley's is a great café
with great coffee,
I turn the page
and raise my cup.

Catch 60

The reason why I write
is to beat the sixty cigarettes
that sixty times a day
push me closer to an early grave
with a headstone marked
'OLAF TYARANSEN
DEAD BARMAN
R.I.P.'

I'm writing the book of my life
and when I reach the final chapter
I'm putting in a happy ending
- immortalising myself with words.

The reason why I smoke
is because I think about death
too much.

Grandmother

for Catherine Fraher

I wonder did she remember
having her religious pontifications
rudely interrupted by an
arrogant sixteen year old
who had recently discovered
existentialism.

She said 'Jesus Christ'
I said 'Charles Darwin'.

She said 'eternal life'
I said something about worm fodder.

We didn't agree to disagree.
She just sat there fuming
and blessed herself.

Now that you are gone
darling grandmother,
I find myself hoping
that you were right
and I'll see you
whenever...

Bad Trip Through the Looking Glass

Terrifying technicolour thoughts
raped and pillaged my mind
and contorted my fragmented face
as I struggled to fish the image out
of the lavish silvery depths
from the inside of my shaving mirror
where I was being kept prisoner
for the simple crime of
                    dropping
                        something.

Two Haikus

Deadline

Unfortunately you may
be dead before finishing
this short line.

Lifeline

Thankfully it would appear
that you survived reading
the words above.

Running Out of Words

There was a news flash
on the radio last week.
Two little girls were killed
in a Des Egan poem
by an IRA car bomb.

The Bishop called it
an atrocity!
The Taoiseach said that he
was outraged!
The PM said that he
was shocked!
The Northern Secretary said
someone would pay!
The Butcher called it
an act of butchery!
A poster advertising a horror film
said that
evil had reached a new low!
And I said nothing because
nobody asked me.

Today there was
another announcement.
A British soldier had
been gunned down in
front of his son.

The Bishop said that he
was shocked!
The Taoiseach called it
an atrocity!
The PM said it was
an act of butchery!
The Northern Secretary said
someone would pay!
The butcher said that
evil had reached a new low!
(he had been to the cinema.)

Somebody asked me what I
thought this time.
I took a deep breath and said that
I was shocked by this
atrocious act of butchery,
evil had reached a new low and
someone should pay!

It's a pity that they
didn't run out of bullets
when everyone else ran out
of words.

Fruitless

The apple at the
bottom of the barrel
is rotten.

It rotted through neglect.
Being only one of many
it had not stood out
although it was the
tastiest fruit
in the barrel.

Disease has destroyed
its once rose red cheeks
and now the worms feast.

Everytime I pull a pint
in the bar where I reluctantly work
I feel like the apple
at the bottom of the barrel
and I can feel the worms
eating my soul.

Senseless

I don't know why
the government needs to know why
and where and when and how
but although I don't see the point,
it's illegal to disappoint
and anyway it's impossible
not to be a statistic
in a country where
there are statistics on people
who are not statistics
so yes - I will reluctantly fill out
the senseless census.

Thoughtless

A thought of mine
that hadn't been thought out
escaped from its brain cell
and avoiding the electric sorting office
shot through the grey labyrinth
past the borders of reason
and across the Rubicon.
Out of my head,
out of my mouth,
out at Elizabeth.

Out of my face now
because she won't talk to me.
Sorry - just a thought.

A Short Poem About Making Love

This is my very first time to
write about my very first time so
this poem is a virgin and
I just used to be therefore
I could never have written this while
I had something in common with it.
Confused?
I was
fourteen.

I hope that you're not expecting
explicit details and erotic images because
all that I can remember was the
embarrassed silence while I worked out
how to find her clitoris.
I felt a bit like Robert Frost.
And the earth didn't move
for either of us

Disappointed?
I was
fourteen.

Waiting for Dole Day to Dawn

I didn't shave this morning
as I wasn't meeting my mother
(or anyone else's)
and besides
I don't usually get
a five o'clock shadow
until about nine.
Anyway, I couldn't afford
the razor blades.

I didn't hear any news today
as I couldn't afford the Times
and I don't read the Star
and the batteries in my
transistor radio are lower
than my spirits
which is probably just as well
I don't want to hear about
inflation and condoms that
I can't afford.

I didn't eat today
not that I wasn't hungry
but when it comes down to
a choice between cigarettes
and a bowl of Sunflower soup,
I can better handle my

stomach growling than
my lungs aching.

There were a lot of things
that I didn't do today because
my money ran out
before the week did
but for now I'll sit guard
over a glass of water
in the Quays before going
back to my cold flat
to wait for dole day to dawn
and to dream about a publisher's cheque
that's greater than my debts.

Bouncer

I don't know this
intoxicated idiot
staggering before me,
poisoning the air with his
bad breath and ugly threats,
waving his well-weathered fists
like a butcher's display
and crunching his black boots
into the car park gravel
ready to reflect my
frightened face
into their steel toe caps
before smashing the image
to pieces.

All I know is that
he wants to spill my blood
over his spilt pint.
I don't ask him why
because I know that he is thinking
why not.

I think of money
and my hurt pride,
lower myself
and meet his challenge.

As he swings his fist
I swear to myself
that the next time
will be for love
not money.

And I will be a Galahad
not a bouncer.

Back to Front

for the girl behind me

When I turn my back
to your front
as we lie at
equal distances from
each other on
restless sheets,
it is not because I
don't want to look at you
or lose my hair in yours
but because I need to feel
your warm breath on my back
fuelling my soul and pushing me
to greater things like an
Eastern wind to a
Westbound boat.

For You

Because I am a man
I am not allowed to cry
(except at football matches).

The respect of my male friends
is stored in my tearducts
and to release these rivers of
respect down my cheeks
would be to lose it forever
(except at closing time)

But my love for you
is what makes me fully a man.
Before you I was just a boy.
Without you I'll no longer be a man.
I'll be a boy again
and I'll be able to cry
(except in the pub).

Neighbours

The people who live
beside me drive a
red BMW but have
no food in their fridge.

And the people who live
beside them drive a
black Mercedes and a
white Golf but have
no fridge.

And the man living
across from them
has a Citroën and
a sit-on lawnmower
(even though his lawn
is smaller than a
postage stamp).

I have no car
and no fridge
and no lawn.
Thankfully none of my neighbours
is called Jones
as I couldn't live
beside myself
with worry.

Nightclub
for Derek and Shane

He's sitting in the darkened corner,
alone with his thoughts and drink.

His mind is paying less attention to the music
than his unconsciously moving head and feet.

Nobody notices him secretly light a joint.
The tip burns red like hellfire as he inhales deeply.

The blue grey smoke lazily escapes his nostrils.
It rises slowly and beautifully, taking his mind with it.

He startles some people by laughing loudly to himself
at a ridiculous thought that has occurred to him.

Nightclubs are full of people like him -
higher than the tangy exotic smelling clouds above them.

Flat Farewell

I'm sitting at a
round (coffee house) table
waiting for my
tired brain to
come alive and fill
the stagnant silence with
the sweet sound of
loving platitudes.

But they won't come.
Blackness. Nothing.

I mustn't love you anymore.

Perhaps I should have
explained earlier
that my average love affair
has roughly the
same durability as a
Duracell.

(I'm sorry now that
I realise your love
doesn't run on
batteries).

Mind Under Matter

I'm not a schizophrenic
but I live two existences
- one in body, one in mind.
I can think what I like
but I cannot do what I like.
That's life.

In my mind's eye I can
beat Mike Tyson
but physically I'm terrified
of paper bags.
That's life.

Or I can paint more brilliantly
than Vincent Van Gogh
even though my paintings are worse
than his hearing was.
That's life.

I write as well
as I can
although I can write better
in my head.
That's my life.

Someday all this
mind under matter

won't matter.
That's death.

Visiting Home

On the rare occasions
that I visit home
my mother scathingly looks
at my Oscar Wilde hairstyle,
my pierced ear,
my Doc Marten boots
and my beautiful red silk trousers
(hand made in Turkey).
But she says nothing.

And my father asks me
'When are you going to grow up
and get a proper job?'
Normally I don't answer
but if I do - he winces
at the sound of
my voice
because it no longer sounds
like his does.

And I know that as soon as
I'm gone (leaving just a
lingering smell of
Cacharel aftershave in
their kitchen).
they're saying to
each other
'Where did we go wrong
with him?'

In Pursuit of Happiness

Finally I've moved up in the world
another step up on society's
Snakes and Ladders board
because today I had a telephone installed
and I can afford to use it if
I smoke less and drink slowly.
Telephones aren't just useful
- they're also good for your health.

Phone wreckers are mindless idiots
but after today it's not my problem,
they can smash as many phones as they like
without causing me to go without
what I can't possibly go without
(Pizzas, taxis, the speaking clock)
- Thank you, Mr Alexander Graham Bell.

My telephone is white in colour
and when it rings, the sound reminds me of
my first introduction to this amazing invention
- old black and white movies.
Nine, two, three, eight, eight, five
(that's my own personal number
and you'll find it in the Book).

I'm so proud to finally own a phone.

I got my first bill today.

It came in a very official looking white envelope
(And I don't get too many of those).
Ninety-seven pounds, sixty-four pence.
Quite reasonable considering that for the last twelve weeks
I've been able to order a pizza
whenever I felt like it.
In fact, I've done some calculations
and if I don't order any more pizzas
I'll be able to afford a cellular phone
that I can carry in my pocket
everywhere and anywhere.

Then I'll really be happy......

Spectrum 1991

Red is the colour
of innocent blood
on a Belfast street.

Orange is the fruit
that can only be eaten
if it's not South African.

Yellow is what you're called
when you're not white or black
in America.

Green is how the Earth
once looked when viewed
from the moon.

Blue is what the sky
used to look like
on a summer day in Dublin.

Indigo has two eyes
having never looked into the heart
of a nuclear explosion.

Violet is only an 'n' short
of perfectly describing
nineteen ninety-one.

Her Today, Gone Tomorrow

The sun sets on my sunglasses
as my hidden eyes set on her
sitting cross-legged on the sand
her blue dress matching her eyes
and putting the putrid sea to shame.

A sudden breeze gently caresses her hair
and as she rises to embrace Nature's warm breath
her loose dress moulds to her body
and the perfect shape of her breasts is as obvious
as I am trying not to be.

I watch her until she goes
leaving behind only an imprint
in the sand and in my memory.
I enjoyed our brief one-sided love affair
- safe, uncomplicated, disease-free, inexpensive.
Tomorrow I'll have another with another
on the beach, in a cafe, somewhere, anywhere.

Somewhere

At this very moment
a baby is being born;
a person has just died;
somebody is making love
(so is somebody else);
a telephone is ringing;
the sun is shining;
a clock is ticking;
it is raining heavily;
a dog is scratching itself;
someone is eating a hamburger;
a shot is being fired;
a song is being sung;
a poem is being read.

No matter what time of
the day or night that
you read this poem
all of these things
are happening
somewhere...

If they are not happening
at this very moment
then I advise you to
stop reading right now
as the end of the world
has come.

Sign of the Times

Sixteen people in all
died horrible deaths
in the fire on the front page
of the newspaper
that I am reading.

A rape victim died
of shock on page two
and my mother almost
went the same way when
she saw page three.

The old man on the next page
was quite fortunate
to lose only a leg
and a wife
in a car crash.

Thankfully nobody else died
in today's newspaper
although there were a number
of rapes, beatings, thefts
and divorces.

I was worried when I read
the article beside the Texaco ad
on the back page

that said the ozone layer
was nearly out of ozone.

I fold the paper
(that a tree died for)
and heave a sigh of relief
that things like this only happen
in newspapers.

Poet Put the Kettle On

I have just put on
my thinking cap and my kettle
and I fully intend to write a poem
before the whistle blows
as the kettle overflows
and floods of steaming water
cascade from the table to the floor
(like a post nuclear war Niagara Falls)
transforming my kitchen into a sauna
or a misty jungle if viewed
from behind the plastic potted plant
that someone once gave me saying
that
I'd never water a real one
which is probably true.

The kettle has boiled.
This is the poem.
All that remains for me to do
is to dot the i's
and cross the t's
while I drink some.

Recreation

People create in order to become
what they have created
when they die.

When Michelangelo died
he became David.

When James Joyce died
he became Ulysses.

When Andy Warhol died
he became Andy Warhol.

When I die I will
become this book.

Take good care of it as
my life is in your hands.